I Read You Green, Mother

Poems by

Will Inman

Edited by David Ray and Judy Ray

HOWLING DOG PRESS

Cover painting, "Near Prescott, Arizona," by David Chorlton

ACKNOWLEDGMENTS
Some of the poems in this book were published in:

Because We Love (Anderie Poetry Press); *Clark Street Review;*
Chiron Review; Freedom Isn't Free; *Images*; *Prayers to Protest:*
Poems that Center & Bless Us (Pudding House Publications);
Ranges (Minotaur Editions); *The Laughing Dog;*
and *The Yellow Butterfly*.

ISBN: 978-1-882863-81-5

HOWLING DOG PRESS
P.O. Box 853, Berthoud, CO 80513-0853
www.howlingdogpress.com

DEDICATION

The Author wishes to thank those who have empowered his work over the years, including Michael Annis, Clyde Appleton, Jennifer Bosveld, Karen Bowden, David Chorlton, Marion Cracraft, Michael Gregory, Carl Hanni, Michael Hathaway, Sherman Hayes, Roberta Howard, Ruth Moon Kempher, Burgess Needle, Mike Nicksic, Michael and Hannelore Rattee, David and Judy Ray, Vernon Rowe, Melissa Tibbals-Gribbin, Jim Watson-Gove, and the editors of diverse publications that have helped bring his poetry to those other friends, his readers. He also wants to thank The Poetry Center of the University of Arizona for their stewardship of the Will Inman Scholarship and The Tucson Poetry Festival for the Will Inman Award.

CONTENTS

PREFACE

When I have asked fellow poets if they could tell me their most basic definition of their work, their answers have often proved haunting. Etheridge Knight told me, "In a word, 'Desperation!'" Will Inman's word was "Always go deeper!" I have never had a chance to ask Jimmy Santiago Baca, but in a letter to Will Inman he once described a goal that included "hurling, catapulting the black stone soul into the abyss... incantating the deadly secrets of life itself, the heartbeat booms of my life shaking and trembling between the lines with beauty, with ever shimmering presence."

In that exchange of letters with Jimmy Santiago Baca, Will Inman expanded his description of his own aesthetic:

> you dive with the black stone into the abyss, you risk all...you create a living tapestry, a whole soul....Taking the total surrender of blind dive...is a hell of a truer, deeper risk than doing it in a drugs or drink destructive plunge...whole galaxies can explode and *still* be part of the larger universal harmony....you're like Whitman: you contain multitudes, and they're not just mobs of globs, they're great dynamic forces, but your kind of awareness also carries whole futures in its unfolding. This has nothing to do with 'being great' or getting credit for genius or any of that, it is organic with hurricanes, earthquakes, the great cries of human pain, the tornadic leaps of hope and fury working in each other.

Will Inman's *Beruf* – his calling – has been to follow wherever the Muse leads, down the dusty road from his little house or to vigorous protests both in his writing and other forms of passionate activism for humanitarian causes.

Judy Ray and I first met Will after we had included a poem of his in our anthology, *Fathers*. Will himself, it seems, had long been something of a father figure for members of his writing workshops, not only in academic sessions during his early teaching, but also in such venues as homeless shelters and prisons. Richard Shelton, famous for his own influential and long-term creative writing workshops in prisons, commented of Will Inman: "Like Whitman he embraces the world: 'Not because I am everything/ but because I am of everything.'"

Sam Hamill, responding to *Surfings: Selected Poems of Will Inman,* wrote: "Will Inman's poetry is informed by a lifetime of compassionate social engagement – from the War Resisters League to working with the homeless – and composed with an educated ear for natural idiom, cadence and image that W. C. Williams or Denise Levertov would admire. This is poetry that is earned, a rich vein in Whitman's grand tradition."

Poetry that is earned! – an interesting concept. I suppose it is possible for a poem to be tossed off in a session of idle reflection, and I certainly welcome and am grateful when one seems to have arrived in this manner as a gift. Some of my favorite poets have written as if crickets and nightingales have shown up at their doors as special deliveries.

Curious as to what Will Inman might offer should we at this moment be engaged in a discussion, I have just opened at random my copy of *Surfings* – the so-called Virgilian dip for inviting Synchronicity and Serendipity.

I open to "What Friend in the Labyrinth" on page 91, and see that its first line is "I stand at the rim of what's accepted...I never expected/ to be grateful to flies."

Good enough! We are poets who welcome the fly and the cricket, the nightingale and the crow, but some of us have had to work harder than others to seek a Thou for an I, a Reader for the fruits of our labor.

Will Inman is one of those. With his unique and intriguing aesthetic, he has earned what the gods have given him, though he still refuses to capitalize the word God.

David Ray
Tucson, Arizona, Election Day, 2008

I Read You Green, Mother

When my father was put in
earth, my mother's grave
grew seventeen years one
month and a day or so, she
lay under english ivy, but I
suddenly saw between those dark
green leaves, other young green
first strange light green leaves I
recognized poison ivy, on my mother's
grave poison ivy, I had to kind of
laugh, but that was not the only other
ivy than english, there was also
virginia creeper, fiveleaf fingers and
non-irritant, with the other vines, that
english death ivy, poison ivy like
irony in her outthrust undefeated
jaws...also two dogwood seedlings
tree of the cross they lynched that
Jesus on, never grew straight again,
grows like a curse and a blessing on my
mother's grave...then...at foot end...
a magnolia sprout, southern lady
pretensions her hillbilly tongue never
quite betrayed her to, still flowering
in the corpse, though...and...near the
head, two small oak sprigs, strength she
somehow never lost...but, most strange
of all, and center, near poison ivy, a
small yaupon, holly, *ilex vomitoria*
which Carolina coastal Indians took
to purge out winter, boiled leaves from
every spring, drank, vomited, came
clean again...

           broke old vessels of past year,

wove new, molded new, made
everything new...

O I read you, Mother I
read your messages, you talk green
to me
          of poisons in the vine,
of gentle green creeping with death,
of lynched saviors, of fallen
pretentions, of oaks
rooting truth strong between teeth,
and of a purge to vomit me of your
death, of your
                    memory, thanks,
Mother, I read you green

I shall not weep at your grave
but I vomit out your death. You
claim from me only that I
live and make things new
I read you, Mother. I
read you green.

Sound is More Subtle Than Footsteps

Sound is more subtle than footsteps,
but most anyone who learns to walk – can
learn to speak.
                    She walks out of a long
corridor of time and in through my ears, her
voice carries her presence, whole and fresh,
her news is good, her spirit strong.
                                    I can
stand back after all those years,
now without grab, and behold her flourishing
                                    and be glad.
Yet I can tell she relishes telling me her
triumphs, as I cherish telling her mine: we
do not need to prove against: and though our
victories may not be **with**, they run parallel
down a common field of meaning.

The invisible rose that opens between us now
once shrank bitter between dark bracts:
took years to let the deep bloom
brave naked air.

I lay no claim on her, my
set-free love floats serene on quiet ripples
of a wide lake, takes a whole sky
to receive

burdens

She carried them to flatlands, to swamp country,
she carried first hills of blue ridge, she
carried huckleberry paths: stone-lined wells,
dug narrow, remembered her innards with chill
water hot summers, swift small streams with
bottoms muddy after swim but clear over stones
when fished, tobacco barns and black gum trees,
deep-hooded bonnets and long gingham dresses
washing, Granny Young settin dusk on the porch
smoking her pipe seeing visions, say **damn!** cut
finger harvesting cabbages sure go to hell –
all these she carried east, this ragged web,
seasons mixed like hogshead cheese – wild
strawberries, june apples, chestnut trees yet
unblighted, snow trudge to school and chill
outhouse, horse shoes flung raising dust
four-dollar hat from Mt Airy, mama dreaming
of wide streets with great mansions, dies a week
later, papa dead drunk not yet fifty, built
first flue-cure tobacco barn in Surry County.

She leaves nine brothers, runs away with two
younger sisters, brushed her teeth with frayed
end of a sturdy twig, broke ice in a porch pan
to wash her face of a morning – she carried
these carried her.
               Society people down east in
Wilmington snickered at her hillbilly brogue,
she'd never eaten **tame strawberries** how they
laughed. Willie grinned weak under fierce
shamed eyes staring, what hills broke in her

ribs, what streams bled.
                         Mountain women
chewed bits of meat, fingered them weaning into
young ones' mouths. Now I carry shreds still
digesting me.

from **The South is a Dark Woman**

1.
The South is a dark woman,
mother of my soul.

Tenderly she got me
from the shadow of a bent wave,
tenderly she left me
at the edge of the surf.

Among all the dunes of white faces,
I never forgot her face.
Her darkness kept cool a place for me
in a rib around my heart
where a dream could mend my waking.

2.
From white columns I would set out,
down cement walks I strode,
from the stone bridge I descended
into ribs of the swamp creek.

There she was with me,
her breath and her presence:
if I did not listen,
she would speak with me;
if my ears did not strain,
I could hear her voice.

Cypress trunks rose brown and tall,
and in the roof of the swamp
cypress needles and vines
wove her green mantle into the blue:
if I did not listen,
I could hear her breathe.

In the shade, cardinal flowers bloomed
and hummingbirds drank sweet honey
at my mother's dark mouth.

At her brown breast, I drank,
to her black mouth I pressed my white ear,
I leaned to her heartbeat,
I yearned to the stroke of her wounded hands.

Though she was forbidden me, I never
forgot her face.

1984: needed: a new Orwell, another future

(latest bulletin from the front)

we have moved our lines forward
one hour into 1984.
fireworks and horns
preceded our advance.
air and sky are clear. we
know very well what
we have laid down behind us:
it awaits us up ahead.
we know it
but prefer to blame it
on the other side or
on the future
               on
somebody else
some place else
some other time:
not ourselves
not here
not now
          please. not now. not yet
but we are already one hour and fifteen minutes
into 1984. Orwell
told us about it, but we
took it inside us
and built it around us.
                   out there somewhere.
we are over one hour into the year we
told ourselves about.
some other time out there
is here already: we are occupied
with a future that was supposed to wait

till we were ready for it
not to happen

we cannot retreat

we can't see that far ahead

we don't know what is now

it's high time for another Orwell. you can't
blame us for 1984. we couldn't
stop it, not even with the latest armaments
how far here can we get
without being somebody somewhere else?
and when we get there,
will we have been here after all?
uh-oh. we are surrounded with a future
that is ourselves as we really are

Alexander's Fury

because my soldiers know my lover
is one of them, they also know i love them all
through him. but this world will not rest
for a man to love another man, not even for a king,
who must beget sons to become kings and rulers
over his people and over those they shall conquer.
since i may not, even as king, rule
with a man at my side,
since it is sons they want of me, sons and power,
i shall lead armies of their sons, my lovers,
to power over all the kingdoms of the world.
we shall get sons not only in Macedonia
but also in Thessaly, in Attica, in Elis, we
shall get sons in Arcadia and in Doris and in Laconia
and in all the states of Greece, we shall get sons
in all the nations of the Mediterranean and of Asia
and of Africa, we shall get sons in the cities of Persia,
and as far as the feet can march, we shall kill and conquer
and teach our ways to all the peoples.
since we cannot stand or lie down
alongside our brothers, our lovers,
we shall hold them under us
we shall kill the brothers
the world will not let us love, and those who live
we shall take as slaves, and of their women we
shall get sons who shall grow up to kill
because they are not allowed to love each other,
and must a few be rulers and many be killed or enslaved,
and all be deceived because they must not see
one another as brothers or women as our sisters. i
must lie to all of them and rule over them
to keep the world safe for getting sons
to kill and be killed lest we become weaklings
and surrender to love.

for this i shall conquer the world
that will not allow me
to love as we want to love.

and i pray to the gods and curse them and look ahead
to a time when our sons shall refuse to go to war
and shall refuse to kill their brothers
and shall stand alongside their sisters
and shall take back the world for lovers.

another kind of pain

he was driving very fast, returning
to Tucson on a rainy night. he
tried
to pass another car. his car met a truck
head on.
o you of broken face, nose
crushed, eyes burst against windshield,
ribs folded around heart and lungs. you
spoke no more words. yet
you left poems
for Melani and me. 'try to publish the best,'
you bade us.
at my homeless workshop, you
sang your poem-songs, played guitar with
fingers not yet broken. your mouth curved
crooked around your melodies with another
pain. you
were not certain who you were.
you went to Guatemala, you sang Spanish
with children orphaned by death squads.
the soldiers of the junta did not catch you.

tomorrow, Melani will bring me your poems. she's
going to seminary. i will read your lines, my
mouth will curve around another kind of pain.

you were not a handsome youth, but once,
after you read poems for homeless people, i
asked you, Do you know how beautiful
you are? your mouth
curved around a smile,
and your eyes went bruised with that other
pain.

a different problem

once, back in the '50s, a leftist friend of mine
was caught by the FBI, locked under Smith Act
charges in Forsyth County Jail. i worked in a
local City Market in Carter's Seafood, small
corner for selling fresh fish and other corpses
from ocean. a trusty from jail stopped by with
an order from the jailer for shrimp and oysters,
clearly not for prisoners. the trusty had a
Lumbee Indian name and looked it — not white,
not black, a man with several races working in his
face. i asked him quietly if he knew Junius: his
muted eyes took friendly fire, he nodded. i
wrote a brief note on wrapping paper, promised the
man that, when he got out, i'd have some fish for
him: he smiled and shrugged.

next time he visited
the fish stall, he had a return note from Junius.
what a victory! contact through a fellow human,
even a stranger, who trusted reach more than risk,
took risk against authority, as mark to his own
self of how to be a brother. the City Chairman
patronized my good intention but put me down
hard for taking extravagant chances which couldn't
help the working class if we were caught.

you and i,
Bill, have a different problem. our friendship is
not political; subversive against death, yes, but
who cares what poets say to each other? our very
label puts bars between us and any we'd care to
touch with special liberating space, that most
infinite life-room, inside.

we will find ways to
outreach being so domesticated and safe. you,
there in jail, i here in my heatless house, are

freer and warmer than most in the world, and we,
o dear brother, have each other, a communion to
build on, a resonance to root futures in, with new
faces and fingers of god to help us travel that
simple mile, together or singly, we move into
one all-varied place.

                     freedom becomes shared choice.

birds when they flew
i heard bellsounds

that day birds when they
opened and shut their wings, when they
flew, I heard bellsounds from them,
together they sounded like rainbows
look, arches of sound came from them,
that day when they opened and shut their
wings, I heard bellsounds, they sounded
springwater speaking earthtones, they
sounded stars shining days from a
well-bottom, they sang soft calls,
good glad calls, they weren't afraid,
they just flew nearby, I heard bells
their singing when they opened and shut
their wings, I heard rainbows of
sound, springwater speaking
to me, I knew without words what was
said, sung, rung, shone, called,
that day birds when they opened
and shut their wings, good glad
calls they sounded, now i'm
telling you, you have to hear with
rainbow ears, with well-bottom
dark, with your own good glad
listening. I heard bellsounds, you
hear what you hear with your own
deepearth ears when birds
fly away near, that day, this day
whichever days they sing I
heard, keep hearing, can
you with your own listening
sounds those wings, bellsounds, star
voices down your own dark
well?

co-dependent

i keep waiting for you
i miss you
i hope you won't show up
you throng me with your absence
i'm glad you're giving up on me
where the hell are you?

you have to get drunk any more
                 to get up courage to come over
i can't stand you when you're drunk
i don't like me when you're drunk
i'm tempted to try to force you
                 to do things you don't want
somehow you never get quite that drunk
i like you when you're sober
i like me when you're sober
you know i mean it when i say, **No**

if only i knew i mean it
you come by when i'm sleeping, you
                 know my resistance is down then
now i have to lock my back door, so
                 you can't appear beside my bed
i fantasize killing you
it's my fault for not sticking to my
     No
i'm going to kill you for **my** weakness?
i miss you
i'm glad you're giving up on me
where the hell are you?

please stay away

who would take your place?

counting

Most days I take walks along a dusty unpaved road
known as the gas line because a high-pressure natural
gas pipe runs underneath the surface.

Yesterday, I
walked along as usual waving at people in vehicles and
speaking to the one or two walkers I met. I counted
responses, one per car or truck, one for two or three
walking together. A small red car turned from Bilby onto
the gas line. A youngish man drove.

'Are you alright?'
'Oh, yes. I wave at everybody.' 'I saw you waving and
thought maybe you needed help.' 'No, I'm fine, but
thanks for caring.'

As he drove away, I registered my feelings
about him. Smallish. Early thirties. Slightly bent but good
nose. Neat close nap of dark hair, parted near but not at
the middle. Thoughtful dark eyes. I wished I'd said more. He
seemed the kind of person who might've made a great
friend.

I counted 37 greetings.
The day before, walking to and from San Paulus,
I counted 52. Most don't respond, but some give wide-arm
generous waves or yells or honks. I say a small prayer for
every 13th greeting. So, it's not just a gas line, it's a way for
brothers and sisters, even at 90 degrees.

Drum House

Sometimes my house throbs like a drum.
It picks up sounds, magnifies them, thrums at me
                                with them,
alien heartbeats trying to take over
inside me.
                I live in an old trailer with a
two-room cabana built on. My neighbor slams a
door, it sounds as if it's in the next room.
Somebody over there slaps feet down off the side
of a bed, I know I have company.
                                Young guy across
the street invites his band over to practice,
only the drums come through, echoing in my walls,
scouring the place with repetitive, merciless
beat. Pick-up passes by on Mossman Road
zoombox turned up loud, I'm sure some strange
crowd is breaking in my west door.
                                Yet, when I'm
outside, I can barely hear the telephone ring.
This house resonance is an internal matter.
When I want to sleep and the drums begin,
forget it.
                Tohono O'o'dham tribe holds pow-wow
miles away on the reservation, I can hear drums
relentless, interrupting — or interpreting —
the moon.
                I mull those muted motions. I lie in my
bed, those far naked hands stroke up and down
my body like startongues, till I bury my head
in the dark loins of sleep.

row drift

i ride the wooden skiff down the slow stream
i find the name of the journey in every curve
on one side a small stretch of sand on the other a straight
      steep bank
the mouth of the flow widens into a delta
where tides surge in and out with the rhythms of the
      moon
a lone cypress stands near the opening of the stream
egrets stalk the shadows and seagulls dive at the small
      fishes
along one side of the stream's mouth is a marsh of wild
      rice, bulrushes, and cat-tails
red-wing blackbirds throng the wild rice sounding
      excited hunger calls
delta opens toward ocean around the small island of
      dunes and sea oats
dolphins dive and leap
turtles dig night out of the dunes and lay their eggs
i cast my line into the sea
my catch is only myself
a low wind mantles the stars

dark flow

teeth of the galaxy
chew dark matter until it glows
blue sky spirals green fern
birds alight on stem
darkness grows wings
i go so far and return
birds chase spirals down
who can fly so far so fast
i am here now sooner than when
dark matter cloaks my shoulders
this is as far as I can know
look with me into the light
and weep

A Reckoning of Emeralds and Curses

Comes a reckoning.
A reckoning with actual living people.
With some dead, now inside me
watching, waiting for the time...
Those outside, going on with their lives,
wearing the wounds I left in them,
secret emeralds, steep curses,
abscesses of pain. Oh, sure, I carry my own
share of such hurts, but those I carry from others
don't cancel out the wounds I've laid
in the reckoners under their ribs, where
every time their hearts beat
something turns more crystal
or rots more bone
                    depending on the individual
strength of the carrier.
                    But strength or weakness
in any one of them
will not change my facing. I
carry in me shadows of emeralds,
odors of pustulance.
                    I will not wait
for later reckoning, though it will come
in its own time. No: I will take
shadows and odors, I will turn them
into dark arms, I
will wrestle that angel
all this night of my waiting
until one of us shall prevail

and then I will climb up and down
the sacred spiral stairs
until reckoning roots into the deepest well
until reckoning vines among furthest stars

and my dark angel will lie close to me again
and we will give birth to god
and god will make peace among emeralds and curses
and they both will shine.

hummingbirds

it is late summer 1939, eastern North Carolina.
a hummingbird crouched on the fallen pear.
the bird was drunk on the fermented fruit. i
caught her easily in my butterfly net. I brought her
into the house, she would fly down to drink honeywater
from a cup I held in my hand. she soon grew weak. i
didn't know I wasn't feeding her enough.
                                    Rosa Wright
stepped from the kitchen into the den. the bright
bird flew from my honeyed finger to the window
where she seemed to catch fire in the sunlight.
Rosa Wright smiled. then the bird flew against the
glass and slid down the pane. a strong look came
across Rosa Wright's dark face. she shook her head
and, without looking at me, left the room.
                                    i'd called
the local newspaper: the item was reported. a knowing
birdlover telephoned to remind me it was against
the law to keep humming birds. i was sad and relieved.
i let the bird go at once. she flew away without
hovering, except in the tingling of my honeyed
finger.
          not long after, stormtroopers cut around
the Maginot Line and headed for Paris. the British
took off from Dunkirk. Hitler was burning all the
hummingbirds in Europe. many, he kept, against the
law, until they starved. so much of the beauty of
the world died with them. he melted down their
feathers to make rockets, the cruel fingers of god
were circumcised with tingling. foreskins of
hummingbird hearts were cut away before the blind
eyes of history.
          but hummingbird hearts, like Shelley's,
refused to be consumed by the fire, they still beat

in the eyesockets of dead god's skull. they have
turned into the seeing of all sufferers;
even their enemies see better by their compassion.

if moon swings out

My glasses fell on the floor
when I bumped the writing board
I'd laid them on.
A scientist declares
the moon is moving away from earth
at the rate of two feet a year.
I was
able to rescue my glasses and the 54-year-old
writing board without stepping on them.
If moon
orbits out of reach, what will summon
and then release the tides?
If I smashed
my glasses, I'd have to drive 'way out
north Tucson. Though I'm driving less
these days, I can't expect friends
to cart me around for everything.
I won't
still be alive if moon swings out to seeming
small. I doubt I'll need glasses to see by
on the other side.
Since leaving us,
Michael Cuddihy gets around without his
wheelchair. Things keep happening to show
he's still around after all.
Maybe he'll
have a talk with the moon before she
gets too far out.

what do you want?

what is it you really want? perpetual
recognition? so, they pass you by, you're not
sweet enough; even when your lines draw blood,
they can't feel the beat, and they're too tough
for your wordy teeth. do your work. they
didn't steal your pencils. only you can
come to terms with your what's so, inside and
outside, and that must happen with
or without
                their approval. so do your work.
don't wait or stew or fret that they might
pass you on the road. if their ways are vital,
that's what matters. do your own work and shut up

To Catch the Truth

Truth
must be played with patience, fish
at the end of a line.
Play and ply, pull
and let line out, then in,
till
bringing in the catch, you find
the hook set fast
in your own jaws

"Why do the nations so furiously rage... Why do the people imagine a vain...?"

7 December 1941. Sunday afternoon.
I descend the stone steps of the campus
clocktower from my room over the archway.
I'm a sophomore at Duke. It's very cold. The day
seems dark. As I step down onto the flagstone
walk, I hear an anonymous shout: WAR!
I see students turn and look across campus
in the direction of the shout's source. I ask
Henry Austin if he knows what's happening.
Hank has just heard the news: Japanese
airplanes have bombed a naval airbase in
Hawaii. We walk on together.

                    Hank and I both
sing baritone in Duke Chapel choir. This
afternoon, we are to sing in Handel's Messiah

I'm seventeen and already an atheist except when
singing the Handel. It's impossible not to
believe in the Presence invoked by that music,
those choruses. Halfway through, during a
quiet passage, Chandler Smith nudges me.
Tall, blond, he can read music much better
than I can. He murmurs, 'I forgot all about
the war!'
                    have mixed feelings, not very
patriotic. I've caught the Nordic obsession and
am a few years getting cured of racism. I've
argued with Hank Austin about all that.
                                        He
enlists and is killed while I'm still at Duke.
He, too, could read notes far better than I
can.
          I've had to make do with words and the

broken flagstones of obsessions. It has taken awhile for me to learn to walk level on uneven ground. Music helps heal my direction. My feet can read music better than I can.

shredding

in her eighties
a live deep grown

walls serene with paintings
shelves rich with original volumes
small sculptures among the books

she modeled in clay
then cast whole

now her hands are too weak to hold the clay

visions strain in her fingers and palms
to shape clay:
                    no more

she can no longer do what she is
her daughter has lost life-seeing.
          her life is no longer living
she takes powders, they
do not go with her separating, she
is trapped between

others do not approve her going

who will allow her the way
and the respect
of parting?

who will attend her knowing
it is ended?

time

that time...this time...
the time comes
                    not rushing
not dragging
                    not needing to argue
not bothering to persuade
                              not naming
its day or hour in advance
                              more often denied
than God is.
                    time flows like a snake
yet like a narrow stream
                    when it reaches you,
it divides, circles you:
                    wet up to your ankles, you cry
perishing with thirst.
                    time
never plays by your rules: you complain that
time never listens:
                    time
doesn't bother to nod its mercurial
                              head.

tarantula

tarantula wears a mustache all over
tarantula may be female or male
once tarantula crawls on your body
       it is like having a hostile continent
       trade places with your feeling safe
tarantula is not eager to bite and is
       as curious about you
       as you are about it
although tarantula's tread makes no sound
       it can look like a tom-tom
       reaching for your ears
such a silence contradicts its source
tarantula lives in a narrow hole
       and can be roused out with water
leave tarantula alone
       not out of fear but in respect
how would you like to live in a
       hole dug for a telephone pole

scan

that red-tailed hawk
floats high overhead, looking,
beak a compass needle
between scanning eyes, wants
smaller furry
or feathered, sends me
a sense of wings with
purpose, of orbit
with claws, mingling
gravity and motive air.
i do not witness plummet,
but my heart
dives, knowing with.

Free Verse

hurry, lookahere son!
in the raleigh paper
billy's poem – it don't rhyme!

ontogeny recapitulates phylogeny

mother, what was i like nursing you
child, you were sompn else

angels laughing

i dive into your darkness,
embrace volcan's smile,
burn with angels,
laughing

nest

blackbirds swim through my eyes
my darkness shudders
i build my nest of flight

greenfield

a fallen log
crosses a narrowness
in the lake
now and then a large ripple
splashes over the log
small fishes
swim in the shadow of the log
or dart into the sun
on the far side
now i am the log
small waves
rinse my nakedness
high in a nearby cypress
strands of grey moss
also make shadows
on the log that i am
an egret flies to an upper branch in the cypress
she is weaving a nest
of long twigs and grasses
with now and then a feather
from wing or breast
a zebra swallowtail swims the breeze
above the lake
azalea bushes dilate the nostrils
of sacred presence
a mussel ploughs the lake bottom
enclosing mother of pearl in the dark
joining the two stretches of the lake
in one rhythm
many are the one.

i am the world

i kept taking on the world and, of course, kept
having to run away. but where was i to go?
the world was as much in front of me as it was
after me, it was under my feet, in the air
over and around me; worse: the world was in me
and throughout me. i finally faced it: i could not
run away from the world. i could not run away
from myself.

     i couldn't keep taking on the world.
but i could change. i could change myself. but
would i change to gain the world's approval? or
would i seek out who i really am and then find
a way to survive, being me?

      first, i had to
accept that i am the world: not all of it, no,
but yet that all the world has a root into my
centermost self. i could hate how the world is
and what the world does to itself because its
falseness is the falseness of ignorant and
mean-spirited people.

      but i could not deny
being rooted, myself, in the center of the world's
problems and possibilities, in what the world and i
can yet become

    together.

      to be a human being in a
faulty world, to be joined in hurt and healing,
is to refuse to be ghettoed in perfection
or in despair.

    i will start fresh where i am
in a world in which genesis
has never ceased, in which tomorrow
teaches and is taught by
today

healing

kneel alongside the pool
of that hurting self.
enter deeper into that center
into that essential elemental health.
chant wholeness under your breath
draw all that hurt and poison within you
let the hurting one rest.
every pore and every cell will sing in your voice.
do not erase the pain from you
let joy replace the hurt.
let quiet ripple across the pool of your face
let quiet ripple across the face of the one who is hurting.
be still and know

arks of our own terrors

how stark a wind, so pale the sun
day leans swift against her dusk
i walk long shadows in the lane
where dark peels light's remaining husk

my eyes grow grit, i rub my sight
a star breaks trembling overhead
my shoulders feel the cape of night
my feet march habits out of dread

trees become persons, faces, threats
familiar road turns feral, wild
i'm in a place with stored regrets
what ancient now chills mild to cold

i cannot run, i can just see,
hear creatures from a primal age
they've leapt from where they hid in me
and danger me with my own rage

i reach toward that naked star
she touches me inside my fear
my inner distance bounds most far
star lifts me raw to waking here

thunder-ache in his shoes

sweat-humid in battered leather, no roar
but rolling pain, how many miles of pave, sole-slap on
concrete,
had he worn into that pair of foot-covers, those miles
weighed in his feet, in his ankles, in the beat of his legs
hard on harder street and road, banging his life out going
from no place to no where, when every place drummed
in his ribs with a crowd of empty.
eyes met his eyes cold or pity drenched.
he found a dime, increased his rich distance
from a meal. he felt earth
turn under his feet, the wide roll through space, sun
sucked at his flesh, he was cooking in his own sweat.

traffic made a dreadsome music around him,
passing him with more how far and how near
to nowhere caring. well. he didn't want pity,
but he did want something to eat, even one
of Casa Maria's peanut butter and jam spreads
on bread with a paper cup of diluted pink juice.
hours yet till mealtime, dry jaws rasping at the count
of time to wait.
his feetbones sang inside his raw shoes, no one
heard but him. he wanted to pray but didn't
know how to believe any more. he looked up
and laughed a low laugh, and for an instant
a yellow butterfly flew in and out of his ribs.

Mulling a Dark Hero

a human can be a great general with no cannon
a human can be a priest without a bible
a human can be a great actor with no lines
a human can make a song without reading notes

who is that with lank hair falling over his eyes
who is it whose laughter makes trees turn and stare
who is it who sees worth in an illiterate just freed
who is it can reverse streams in their beds

i never knew this man but he ancestors me yet
his darkness has no awe before my pale skin
he looks into me for kinship i had not suspected
his and my white ancestors begot his vision
                                with their hate

now, learning of their meanness, i lean to his arms
he looks at me, sees my hunger, and laughs
abashed, i turn away. he laughs again
and reaches to touch me. i catch fire

i cannot trot back across all those years
i have to travel that road inside me
i carry walls sown inside me, grown in me
from back when. i walk through them and laugh

he hears my laugh, and his eyes slant mull
he brushes dark hair from his eyes, he
looks and laughs. he's one of his own time
laughing with me, he brings back when into view

daemoninmaniana

went to his house, papers all over the floor,
he said they were poems, his wings, he said, i
couldn see how anybody could fly'd let his wings
be trampled underfoot like that, dust on everything,
flyspecks and cobwebs on the windows didn't look as if
they'd ever been washed, cobwebs hung from the beamed
ceiling, dirt and gravel thick enough to plant in
on the kitchen carpets, dirt on refrigerator doors,
clothes piled top of piles of poems on a long table,
clothes piled on two or three kitchen chairs, six
pairs of shoes around under the kitchen table, he did
seem to wash his dishes but then let'em pile up in
the drying rack to catch more dust, had to wash most
of'em again before he could use'em, kept a bucket
with a toilet seat balanced on it, plumbing was
busted, he pretended it wasn't there, nor the piss
jar next to the steps to the trailer part, kept his
bed unmade or about half-made up in one trailer room,
with two rooms full of books and papers, boxes full,
stacks, two crammed file cabinets, he said he felt
he was owned by his stuff, he didn't own it, didn't
know what to do with most of it, hated to have friends
see the piles of stuff, dirt, clutter, only spiders
he killed were brown recluses and black widows, he
left the others to take care of any bugs except for
those of the FBI, they'd take more than spiders. he
figured if he fell in love he'd have to break down
and clean up the place, kept avoiding that, edging
toward too old for either, then he wouldn have to
bother, so he wrote, wrote, made love to his poems,
to the god in him, the devil, said maybe they were
like Adonai and Elohenu, both faces of one god, only
sometimes male, sometimes female, sometimes both,
depending on what **he** was at any given cosmic instant

in time, said even he was at any given cosmic instant
in time, said even in that dry, dustridden place,
writing would bring in ocean, high mountain, oracle
trees, dolphins, coyotes, and an occasional beautiful
boy or girl to build his soul fresh around, said he
never stopped giving birth to himself and that
anyone who read his work with his marrow could not
cease being born and reborn and borning others.
then made me step outside his east door, irises
sang with calendulas, hollyhocks spoke oracles to
hummingbirds, grapevines, apricot trees, figs –
stole desert water to stand up to sun, his hands
proved him every day what can be wrought in desert
he tracked all that dirt into his trailercabana,
all those words rooted in his tongue rooted in
earth when it fills his throat it will all sing

earth   potter

only one was known
to remain among the peoples.

found along an ancient roadway, earth potter
was   shaped like   a person

a bit of smooth stone
    nose and cheeks of broken pot
body of kilned clay

carrying promise of lasting waking
lasting connection with all beings and things
in earth potter was no death, though changes
lay hidden in its meditated being

tribal members held it both with familiar hands
and with   awe
as might be embraced a   grandparent

children were urged to keep observant
in case another potter might be found
to inspire the peoples

but remains in the one
a secret presence small but powerful
with to-be-divined portents
and   potentials

each person carries potter essence
a reminder in everyone

every person is a ditch of sacred potters
earth wakes wondrous in each

a brief man

After lunch in Voc, Joe
blows on his flute.

Alberto, a brief man with
red hair and a Spanish name,
walks into the cubicle of
sound.

He stops, looks at Joe,
then moves toward the flutist,
wonder and caution
mingling in his face.

When he stands directly before Joe,
he reaches a hand, lays it on Joe's arm,
stares lotus into Joe's eyes.
Joe, looking into Alberto's looking,
plays,
those sounds flute under the deep ceiling
Vocational dissolves into lotus

Alberto
turns and smiles at Jeanne and me, then
nods toward Joe

He walks away slowly, his old man gait
halt under loose trousers.

By his I.Q., he's retarded

But what happens behind Alberto's eyes
when that flute
sounds?

tapes of memory keep unwinding

The moon glowers from between two dark brick
buildings. It's not quite full and stares down
rock still. I'm outside a factory. Bright lamps
make caves in the darkness. A train on a short
track is moving giant hogsheads of tobacco on
flatcars to factory loading docks. Silhouettes
of men in coveralls and caps with stripes that
can only now and then be seen – move in
pantomime at loading platforms. I approach
three of the men on one dock and speak to them
of joining the union. They glance at each other:
one coughs, one looks away, the third mutters,
**We can't talk about that on the job, we'll be
fired if we're caught.** I move away. Recognize
two other men, black brothers whom I knew years
ago as union members. I want to remind them
it's time long overdue to restore union in this
plant. They both look hard at me, but I see now
they don't know me. I've aged, but they haven't
changed in forty years. A white foreman dressed
in business suit comes out on the platform. He
gives a sharp look at the two, then stares at
me. **You have no right to keep me alive in your
memory,** he shouts. **I'm a christian – what on
earth am I doing in your communist head? Look
here, you! I'm dead now. Let go of me!** He glows
suddenly, then disappears. The loading dock
fades. So do the train and the workmen and the
cave of light. I'm alone somewhere else. It's
raining. A stray dog sniffs my ankles and moves
away into the night. What am I doing out here?
Huh. That is not the same moon I saw a little
while ago. This one is only a third full and is

caught in the branches of a mesquite. This is
another town. A different life. Why won't that
other life let go of me? What have I left undone?

Alzheimer's Wife

He's forgotten who I am. He
seems to believe his Mom
has left him with me.
                    It's all day,
every day, and lying half asleep
all night, every night.
                    He doesn't
like to undress in front of me.
When I make him take a shower, he
gets all shy and ashamed, says
he doesn't like to get naked
before a stranger.
                    I have to
wash him, scrub him all over,
but I can't **reach** him.
                    I wish
just for a few minutes I could
discuss the situation with him.
He was always so insightful
whenever we faced a dilemma.
Now I must think for us both. I
feel grafted onto him. I have
no life left of my own.
                    I used
to think shells were beautiful
when the mollusk was gone.

Every minute! Every last minute!
I can't even go to the toilet or
take a bath without – damn! It's
not fair. It's just not fair.
                    I'm
his slave, but he acts as if I've

enslaved **him**. I catch myself
praying he – God! We were in love
47 years till this. It's just...

dusk between

ocean   breathes sky. sky dances. earth
turns, swimming. roundings on roundings.
late sun early dark. lover bends to lover.
wave curls to wave, lip brushes lip.

season crosses season. time-pearl
dissolves in milk-dark. death's
a child with soiled clothes, crying
to be changed. mother

doesn't like the stench. god
has to swap diapers. changes child
instead. what late bird
beats wings down coastline, waves

are lost feathers along with moon
scatterings. earth has turned sun
under. pinfeathers spark night.
a thousand hatchling turtles chant.

my latest role

i told my best friend i felt i was cast
in the role of an aging man in a play but that
when they ended its run, i couldn't shake the part.
instead, i've continued to grow older.
                                    i look at myself
and murmur, 'What am I doing taking on that way?
I'm not old. I've never been old. Why can't I just go back
to being plain old Will? – well, I mean...'
                                    i have to laugh
at how words can turn on you.

                        sometimes this carries the play
too far. if i don't care to relieve myself frequently, i
wet my pants. now that's just too damn much – the idea! even
in the actual play, i never had to pee my pants.
                              talking about gifted
performances! such a thing as going too far even in a
good cause.
          for instance, i have to be careful not to fall out of bed.
you see, i'm living in a retirement home for men. but who says
i'm retired?
          can't you understand i'm still playing my old man
role? damn show is a longtime over, but i seem to be cast
for life. i shuffle, i walk bent, my voice croaks, i can't read
worth a damn. at this rate, they'll soon publish my obituary,
and what in hell will i do then?
                              it'd all be downright funny
if it weren't so real. will somebody kindly tell the role
        casters
i'm really still me, not just one more old fart trapped in a
dragging future?
                hey! what do you mean? i'm just in denial?
don't you think i know what's with me?

enemy territory

these continents ride and override each other.
their timpani is a clashing of stones, their winds
are hissings of lava erupting into lakes. they
are populated with pasts and futures very present
yet quite beyond reach.
                              how i long for them! how i
curse their nearness! they groan in me like walls
i see and hear drumming with worn light years.
they could not betray me had i not abused them.
guilt and contrition do not strip away their
sidereal distances. a delicious meal gone cold.
i approach them with these words. words. these
words. shreds of a once-rich life-flag.
                                        promissory
notes i cannot redeem to myself. now continents
slide and shove. what were streets and firm paths
now shiver and heave out of place. salt puddles
mark my passing. what were reeds and bulrushes
have come scrags. god leaves love-notes of dust
and dung.
                    this is an opera, and i'm playing the lead.
i'm an old man, and my role won't let go of me.
people applaud: wind in the shutters. lava
hisses under the audience. what kind of reviews?
i think i'll ask for a new part. i won't insist on the lead.

in the living weft

when she took up strands, as she wove
patterns, she bled soul into the weave, she
kept inside what she was creating. so it was
with humans and other creatures: she
lived in them, they
lived in her.
                  she met the black minister
on the back steps of a dead friend they both
were mourning. later this white sister
was baptized in his church by the black
preacher who couldn't read: his children
would read bible stories to him. he created
his sermons from them. she
was not churchy, but she rejoiced
in spiritual creatures.
                        deer
fed at her back door. their trust
fed her. pet animals made home with her.
she and her sister were kin to the marrow.
when she died, the preacher
led her funeral.
                    rest well.

mesquite   mother   territory

aluminum cans are not always easy to retrieve
from under mesquite trees, the branches of which
tend to drag the ground: they wear thorns and
grow in knotty thickets. i poke my stick in
at a can under the dragging limbs, the can
bounces off a stem and caroms closer to the trunk.
i have to find a way in through branches to
reach the can with fingers that by now are
scratched and bleeding from thorns. mesquites
belong to a tribe often beaten in battles with
cattlemen and utility people who lay gas lines
and string wires, but the mesquite tribe has
never surrendered and still considers desert its
own mother territory. mesquites grow along the
chainlink fence between me and neighbors on both
sides, but it's not **my** land they're marking –
where **they** grow is **theirs.** sometimes i trim
their bottom limbs, but that doesn't bother them;
they still send roots as far as they need to for
water, and they still drop sticky bean pods on
my pick-up's windshield. i do find a lot of cans
under mesquites along the gas line and bleed some
getting them, but i don't resent the trees or even
their thorns. they're my only real firsthand
connection with indigenous souls, they remind me
i'm not a conqueror, only a temporary pestilence.
mesquites outnumber me and my kind, and they have
plenty of time. unless and until we decide to
get our aluminum and other ores with something
noisier than a stick. then, well, even mesquites...

as shadow flows on rock

this old goat stands in mountain shadow
watching young hunters, how they creep and
crawl, how they crouch behind boulders, mutter;
how they shift their guns. the barrels flash
sun.
       he's not afraid of them, though they
sadden him. they ugly the air, even on this
high pure place. he watches. they approach,
but they're not really any closer: their own
noise, muted as it is, congeals around them,
shutting them in.
                  he leaps. he steps slow. they
cannot see him in shadow, though now and then
one thinks he sees movement. one hunter shoots.
the others curse that sound.
                            the old goat jerks
his chin. if he were a man, he'd do much as
they do. if he were one of several, he'd act
severally. but this goat is alone. hunters
killed his mate and took her young one to tame.
the old one has only himself, and, may be, some
future mate.
            alone for now, he flows in shade
as shadow flows on rock. the hunters stumble,
stones without roots in the mountain.

those i have known living

those i have known living who are dead
are not dead in me i cannot reduce them
to bones they speak to me as unexpectedly as
they ever did, they have not dissolved in
forgotten situations, they attend my ongoing
dilemmas, it is not fair or just i have made
them so much a part of me they had no chance
to say **No** even now when they contend with me
it is my own contention they embody they do
help me stay honest within me even dead they
will not let me lie, not long anyway, to my
self oh but how i'd like to give up honesty
and their shadow voices for one real look
into their eyes, one bruising brush of their
armhairs against mine again, not from
nostalgia, no, but because their living
presence gave me more true learnings of my
self than their ghosts ever could or can

all i can say now in answer to this pain
is that there are others, still living, i
must not abuse them with my independence
i must be willing to take the dangerous
bruises of their present beauty and ignorance
and prejudice and stubbornness, not making
mere allowance, but because they're alive
and i love them and need them and because
they're as fragile as ghosts and as untouchable
even when we touch we live in each other

didn't i always know the fierce hold of your
hands on my heart keeps creating the beat?

ABOUT THE AUTHOR

Will Inman was born on May 4, 1923, in Wilmington, North Carolina. He graduated from Duke University in 1943, then held jobs in a shipyard, a trade union, libraries, universities, and a facility for the disabled. Among other leadings he was an activist in the War Resisters League and other organizations, and was writing all during this time. He co-founded and edited the literary journals *Kauri* and *New Kauri*. After some years in New York City, Inman moved to Tucson where he worked with the developmentally disabled and led writing workshops for the general community as well as for people in homeless shelters and prisons.

Will is author of several chapbooks as well as the 2005 collection, *Surfings: Selected Poems* (Howling Dog Press). Since that book he has brought out two more chapbooks, *Ranges* (Minotaur Editions) and *Leaps of Hope and Fury* (Pudding House).

Extensive archives of his published and unpublished work are held in the libraries of Duke University and the University of North Carolina Wilmington. These manuscripts include a long novel and a memoir as well as much other material worthy of the attentions of scholars and publishers.